Y0-CUO-885

j 921 Pontiac
Voight, Virginia Frances.
Pontiac, mighty Ottawa Chief
DOWNTOWN   ocm02346733

71019200031 8163

PONTIAC
MIGHTY OTTAWA CHIEF

BY VIRGINIA F. VOIGHT

ILLUSTRATED BY WILLIAM HUTCHINSON

GARRARD PUBLISHING COMPANY
CHAMPAIGN, ILLINOIS

For
Gregory Cohen
A Boy Who Likes to Read

ALICE MARRIOTT and CAROL K. RACHLIN of Southwest Research Associates are consultants for Garrard Indian Books. They are presently joint artists-in-residence in the Division of Language Arts at Central State College, Edmond, Oklahoma.

MISS MARRIOTT has lived among the Kiowa and Cheyenne Indians in Oklahoma and spent many years with the Pueblos of New Mexico and the Hopis of Arizona. First woman to take a degree in anthropology from the University of Oklahoma, she is a Fellow of the American Anthropological Association, now working with its Curriculum Project.

MISS RACHLIN, also a Fellow of AAA and of the American Association for the Advancement of Science, is a graduate in anthropology of Columbia University. She has done archaeological work in New Jersey and Indiana, and ethnological field work with Algonquian tribes of the Midwest.

Library of Congress Cataloging in Publication Data

Voight, Virginia Frances.
   Pontiac, mighty Ottawa Chief.

   SUMMARY: A biography of the Ottawa patriot and war chief who united the Great Lakes tribes against the intruding British, laying siege to Detroit in 1763 in a culmination of what has come to be known as Pontiac's Conspiracy.

   1. Pontiac, Ottawa Chief, d. 1769 — Juvenile literature. [1. Pontiac, Ottawa Chief, d. 1769. 2. Ottawa Indians — Biography. 3. Indians of North America — Biography] I. Hutchinson, William M. II. Title.
E99.O9P668   973.2'7'0924 [B]   76-25244
ISBN 0-8116-6613-1

Copyright © 1977 by Virginia F. Voight
All rights reserved. Manufactured in the U.S.A.

Contents

1 An Ottawa Boy 7
2 Chief Pontiac 17
3 Pontiac Accepts a Red Belt . . . 24
4 The Battle at Fort Duquesne . . . 30
5 A Meeting in the Forest 36
6 Trouble with the English 46
7 War Plans 54
8 A Victory for Pontiac 60
9 Pontiac Buries the Hatchet 69

The Ottawas

Pontiac's people, the Ottawas, were Algonquian Indians who lived in villages close to the Great Lakes.

The homes of the Ottawas were large cabins made of pole frames covered with bark and mats made of rushes.

In summer the Ottawas grew maize, beans, and peas and fished and hunted small game nearby. Summer was also the time for making war on other tribes, for celebrations, and for games.

After the crops were harvested in the fall, the Ottawas left their permanent homes and moved to the tribal hunting grounds, where they lived in tepees and hunted deer, bear, beaver, otter, and buffalo.

In the spring, the Ottawas tapped the maple trees in the forest for syrup. Then they broke camp and headed for the nearest fort, where they traded their furs for supplies. After the trading was over, the Ottawas returned to their villages to start the year's activities again.

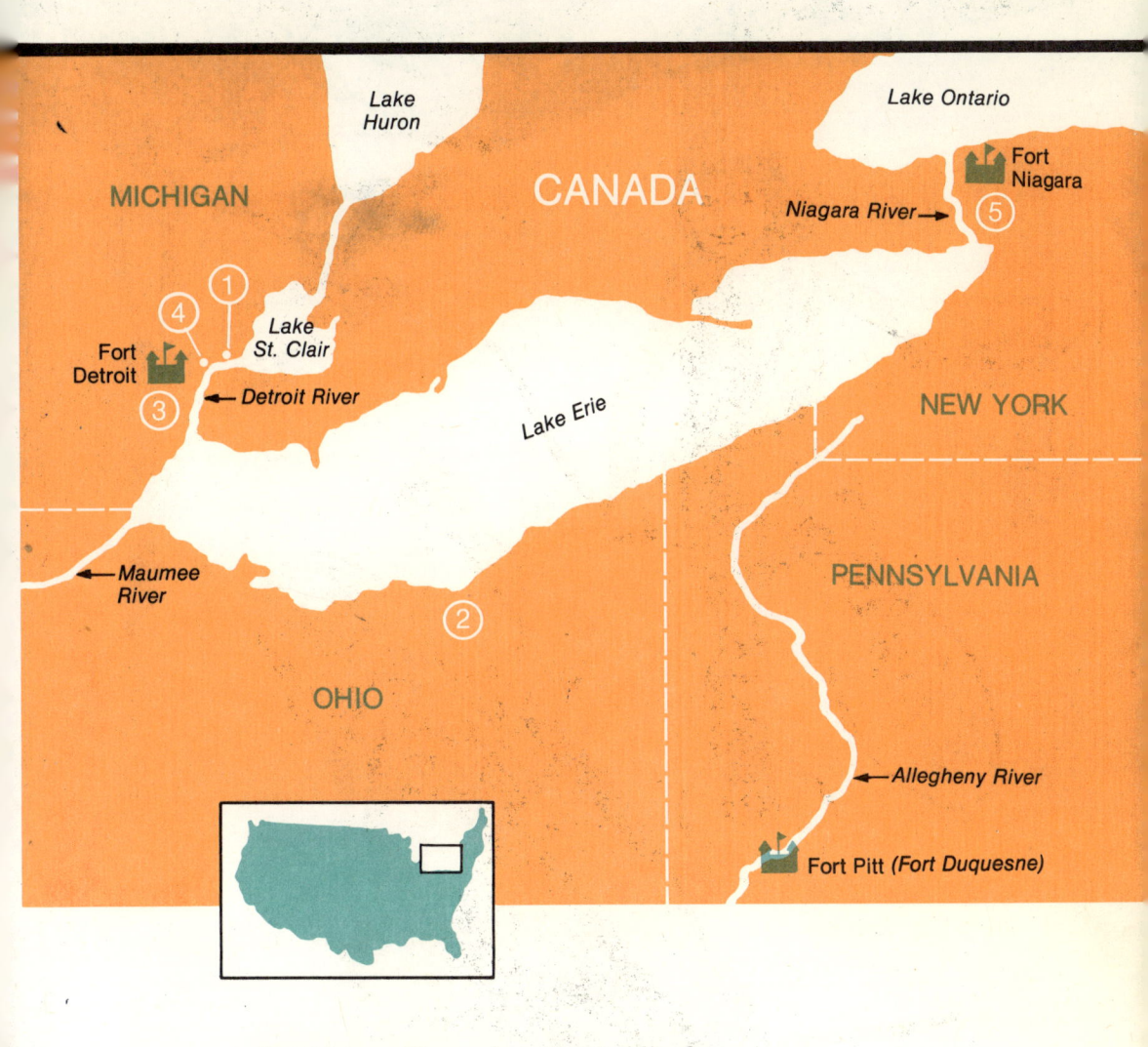

1. The Ottawa village where Pontiac lived

2. Where Pontiac tried to stop Major Rogers and his Rangers from entering Ottawa lands

3. Where the Ottawas and other Indian nations met in council to plan a war on the British

4. Where Ottawa warriors and British soldiers met in the fierce Battle of Bloody Run

5. The cliffs above the Niagara River where Pontiac's men wiped out a British army wagon train

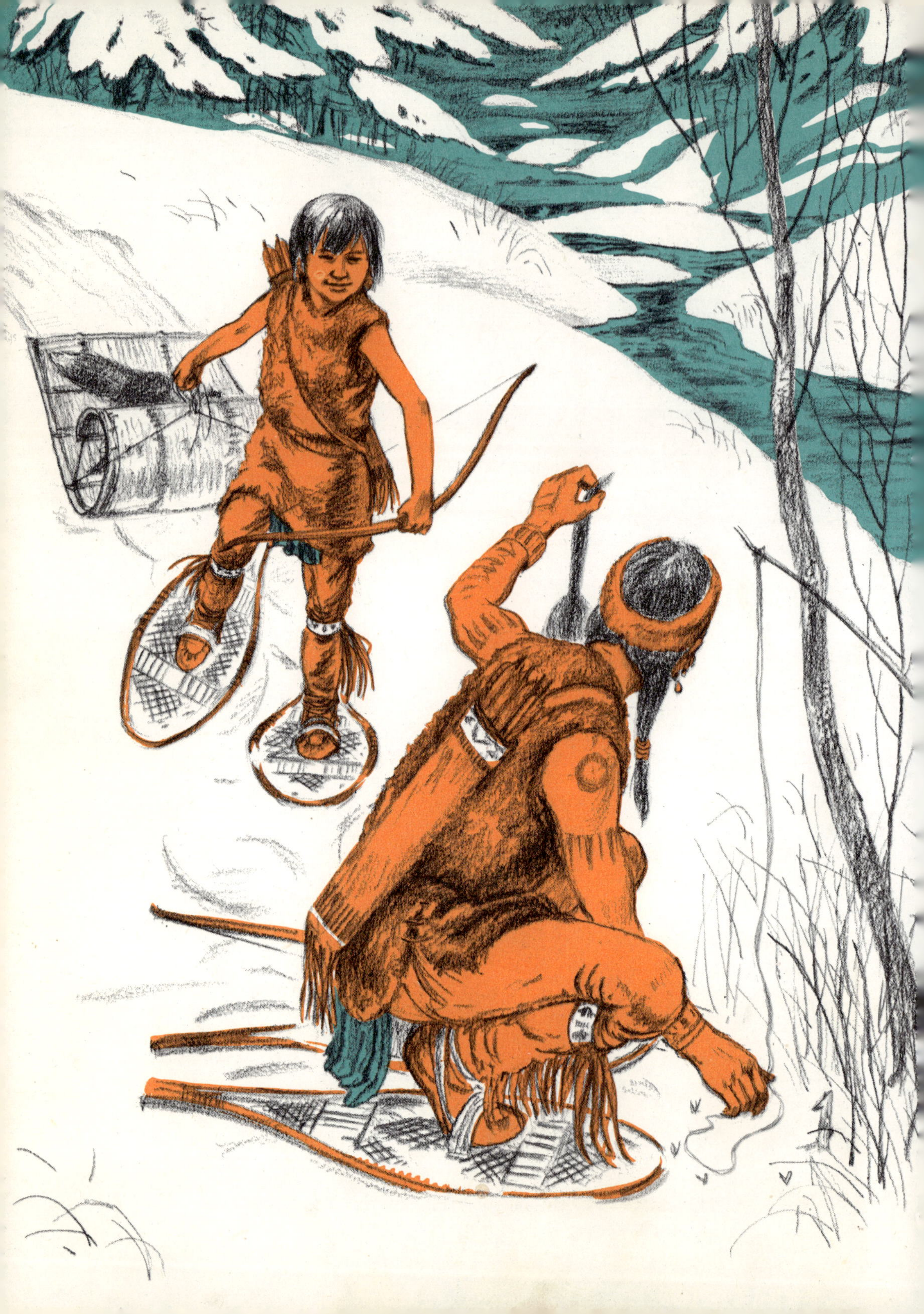

1
An Ottawa Boy

It was winter in the northern forest. The year was 1735, as white men counted time. Ten-year-old Pontiac and his father were checking their traps. The tall Ottawa brave pushed ahead on his snowshoes. Pulling a birchbark toboggan, Pontiac snowshoed behind him. In his other hand he carried his bow of hickory wood.

The first trap held the body of a black fox. In the next trap, by a brook, was a dark-furred mink. Pontiac put the dead animals on his toboggan.

"Our catch is good today," he said thankfully.

The fur they trapped was like money to the Ottawas. They traded it at the French fort at Detroit. There they could buy many things they wanted from the white men.

Pontiac hoped that by spring there would be enough fur to buy him a gun. His father owned a fine French gun, but he often saved bullets by hunting with his bow.

"We must not depend too much on goods that we get from the traders," he told Pontiac. "Before the first white men came here, many snows ago, our people made everything for themselves. I wish it was still like that. That is why I have taught you to make arrowheads of stone."

Pontiac listened, but he still wanted a gun of his own.

His father stopped to study some tracks in the snow.

"Do you know what animal made these?" he asked.

"A moose," Pontiac said quickly.

Like all Indian boys, he had studied the animals that lived in the forest.

"Food is low at our camp," said his father. "If we can kill this moose, we will have meat enough for many days." They started to follow the moose trail. An angry roar made them stop short.

"Here he comes!" Pontiac shouted in terror.

The moose had backtracked on the trail to wait for them. As he charged out of some thick pines, he looked so big that his antlers seemed to shut out the sun.

Pontiac was frightened, but he remembered that he was an Ottawa hunter.

And his family needed meat. Breathing hard, he pulled an arrow from his shoulder quiver.

His father's arrow was already singing through the air. It hit the moose but did not kill it. Before the hunter could shoot again, the moose was on him. Its antlers tossed him high. Pontiac's father sailed through the air and crashed into some bushes. The moose rushed to kill him with its sharp hooves.

Pontiac ran forward and took careful aim with his bow. The arrow hit the great animal's heart. The moose went down in the snow. "Ki-eee!" Pontiac shouted.

His father got to his feet. He was shaken and cut but not badly hurt. He laid his hand on Pontiac's shoulder.

"You are a brave hunter," he said proudly.

Ottawa hunters always made an offering to the spirit of any animal they killed. Pontiac hung the ears of the moose on the branch of a tree.

"Oh, brave moose!" he cried, "I am sorry that I had to kill you. Do not haunt me, moose."

The father and son returned to their winter camp with their catch. No other wigwam stood nearby.

Pontiac's father gave the rolled-up moose hide to his wife. "From this hide you can make many moccasins," he told her.

Pontiac helped his mother and sister stretch the hide between two trees. His mother must scrape and soften it before she could make moccasins.

There was a small stone fireplace inside the birchbark wigwam. Pontiac's mother melted snow in her kettle and put in a big piece of moose meat. She had no salt. She seasoned the meat with maple sugar, and she added two handfuls of dried wild onions.

When supper was ready, the family gathered around the fireplace. Each had his own wooden bowl and spoon.

"We are thankful to have a brave young hunter in our family," Pontiac's grandfather said.

Pontiac's mother smiled across the fire. Pontiac could not help but be proud.

At bedtime everyone climbed on the sleeping platforms. Pontiac pulled his warm bearskin blanket over his little brother and himself. It had been a good day! He was smiling when he fell asleep.

Pontiac had been born in an Ottawa village on the bank of the Detroit River. His mother was an Ottawa woman. His father was a Chippewa who had come to live with his wife's people. These two friendly nations claimed land around the Great Lakes. They belonged to a group of tribes that were known as the People of the Calumet. They believed that the first redstone pipe, or calumet, was given to them by the Great Spirit. The men smoked their pipes at councils and on all important occasions.

In future years, Pontiac's country would be known as the state of Michigan.

When spring came, Pontiac's family returned to their Detroit River village. The rest of the Ottawas returned from the winter hunt also. The summer wigwams of this large village were built with frameworks of poles. Over the poles were laid mats made of rushes. That spring Pontiac helped his father make a new birchbark roof for their wigwam.

When the roof was finished, Pontiac's father told him to shoulder the fur pack. "We will go to the fort and do our trading."

A French soldier was guarding the gate at Fort Detroit.

"Hello, puppy," he greeted Pontiac. "You've grown tall during the winter."

Pontiac straightened his shoulders. A boy who had killed a moose was too old to be called "puppy"!

Inside the walls of the fort the two Ottawas walked along the street to the trader's store.

"Greetings, brother," the French trader said to Pontiac's father.

He handed him a cup of rum. To Pontiac he gave some candy.

The first French soldiers and traders had come to Detroit 34 years before. Antoine de Cadillac, a great soldier and

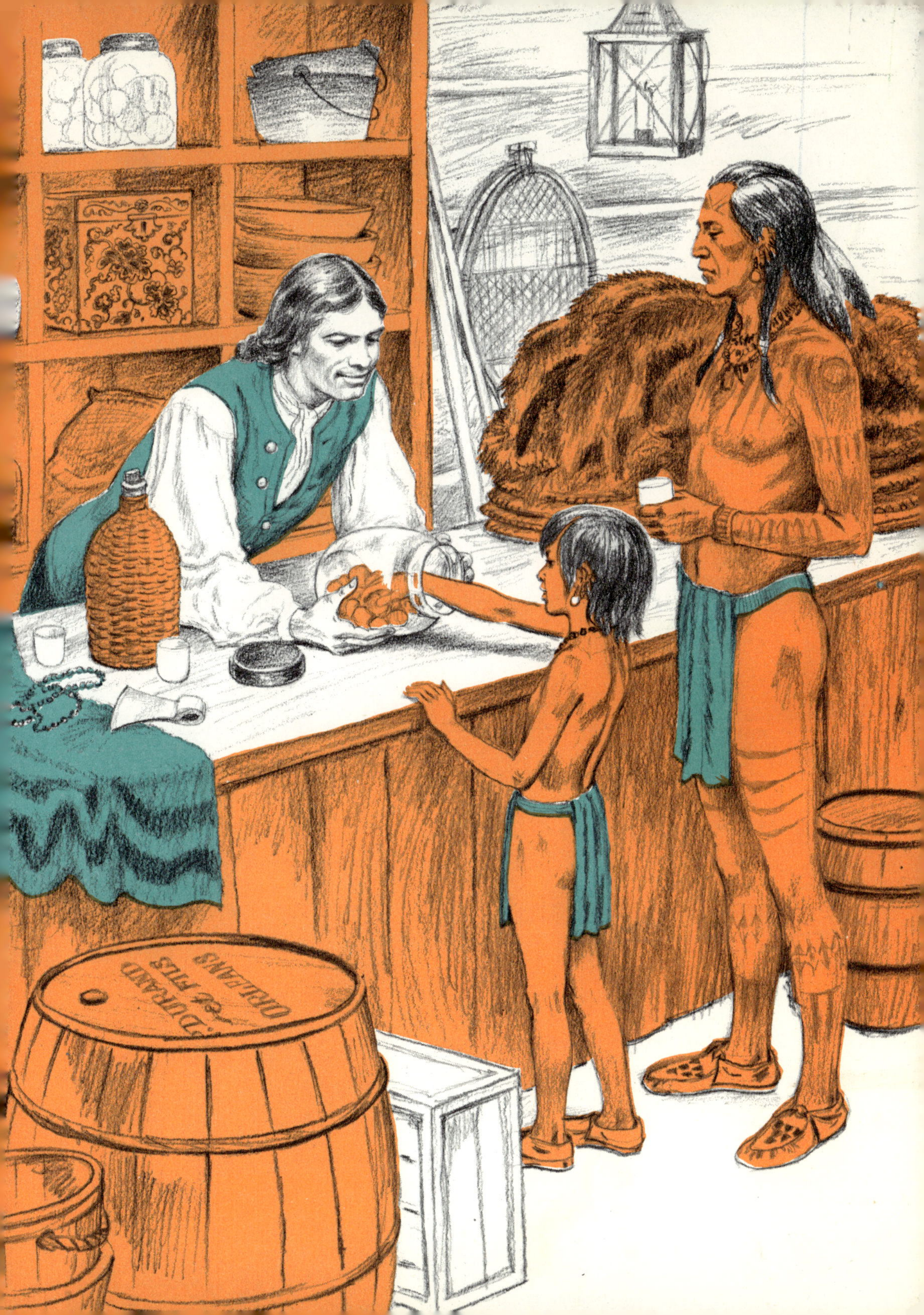
D'URAND
& FILS
ORLEANS

explorer, had built Fort Detroit. Ever since, the French and the People of the Calumet had been friends.

The trading began. Pontiac's father held up each fur, and the trader gave him a fair price for it. When the Ottawas left the store, Pontiac had a new gun. In a blanket shoulder pack, he carried bags of gunpowder and bullets. There were blue cloth for his mother and ribbons for his sister.

"Are all white people as friendly as our French brothers?" Pontiac asked.

"No," said his father. "The English are bad people. They fight with our French friends. They try to steal our land. Let us be glad that they live far away, toward the rising sun."

Pontiac held his new gun tightly. "If the English ever come here, I will help to drive them away," he promised.

2
Chief Pontiac

It was September, many years after Pontiac's father had given him his first gun. Pontiac now had two young sons of his own. The three had come to Lake Erie to fish. Red maples burned among the tall green pines on the lake shore. Indians usually went on the warpath at this season, but today everything seemed peaceful. Pontiac's canoe floated lightly on the blue water.

Pontiac was a strong, broad-shouldered man. His dark face was usually proud and thoughtful, but today he laughed and joked with the boys. They pulled in one fish after another.

When the sun sank behind the trees, Pontiac pulled in his line. "We have enough fish now," he said.

He turned the canoe into a stream that ran into the Detroit River.

The canoe slipped along without a sound. This was the time of day when deer came to the water to drink. But there was not a deer to be seen, nor any other animal. This made Pontiac uneasy. Had something frightened the animals into hiding?

Suddenly an owl hooted deep in the woods. This owl did not sound quite right to Pontiac.

Another owl call came from far away. Pontiac felt sure that he was not hearing real birds. War parties often used bird calls for signals.

Quietly he sent the canoe to the bank of the stream and stepped out.

"Wait here," he whispered to his sons.

Silent as a shadow he moved into the forest. He climbed a hill and looked around. On the lake shore below him, a number of canoes were drawn up. There were strange warriors on the beach.

Then Pontiac crept down the hill and through the woods to the beach. He hid behind a big log where he could hear what the strangers were saying. They belonged to a tribe from the far north.

More and more canoes kept coming to the beach. The warriors talked together about capturing Fort Detroit. They were planning to kill all the French and steal the goods in the trading store.

Pontiac knew that there were only a few soldiers at Fort Detroit. The Ottawa and other neighboring tribes were friendly, so the French had not built a strong fort. It should be easy for this large war party to capture it.

War parties usually attacked at sunrise. Pontiac had time to warn his French friends! He crawled away from the beach and raced back to the canoe.

"Push off!" he cried to his sons. The canoe sped along the stream into the Detroit River. As soon as he reached the Ottawa village, Pontiac told the head chief what he had seen. The chief sent a messenger to warn the French.

The Chippewa and Potawatomie villages stood nearby. A little further away were the wigwams of the Hurons. The Ottawa chiefs sent messengers to these friendly tribes. They asked the other warriors to help them defend Detroit.

Pontiac was not yet a chief, but he had made a name for himself as a brave and wise warrior. Tribes from the north and east had invaded the Ottawa hunting grounds before. Pontiac had taken a leading part in fighting them off. And so now the Ottawas were ready to follow him.

The Ottawa war party, together with the Chippewas and Potawatomies, hid in the woods between the fort and the lake. Near sunrise they heard owls hooting here and there in the forest. The enemy warriors were keeping in touch with one another as they moved forward.

The light grew stronger. Then suddenly Pontiac saw one of the enemy creeping from tree to tree. He shouted his war cry, and the Ottawas blazed away with their guns. The Chippewas and the Potawatomies opened fire also. The invaders fought fiercely, but slowly the others drove them back to the lake. Only a few of the enemy escaped. The quick

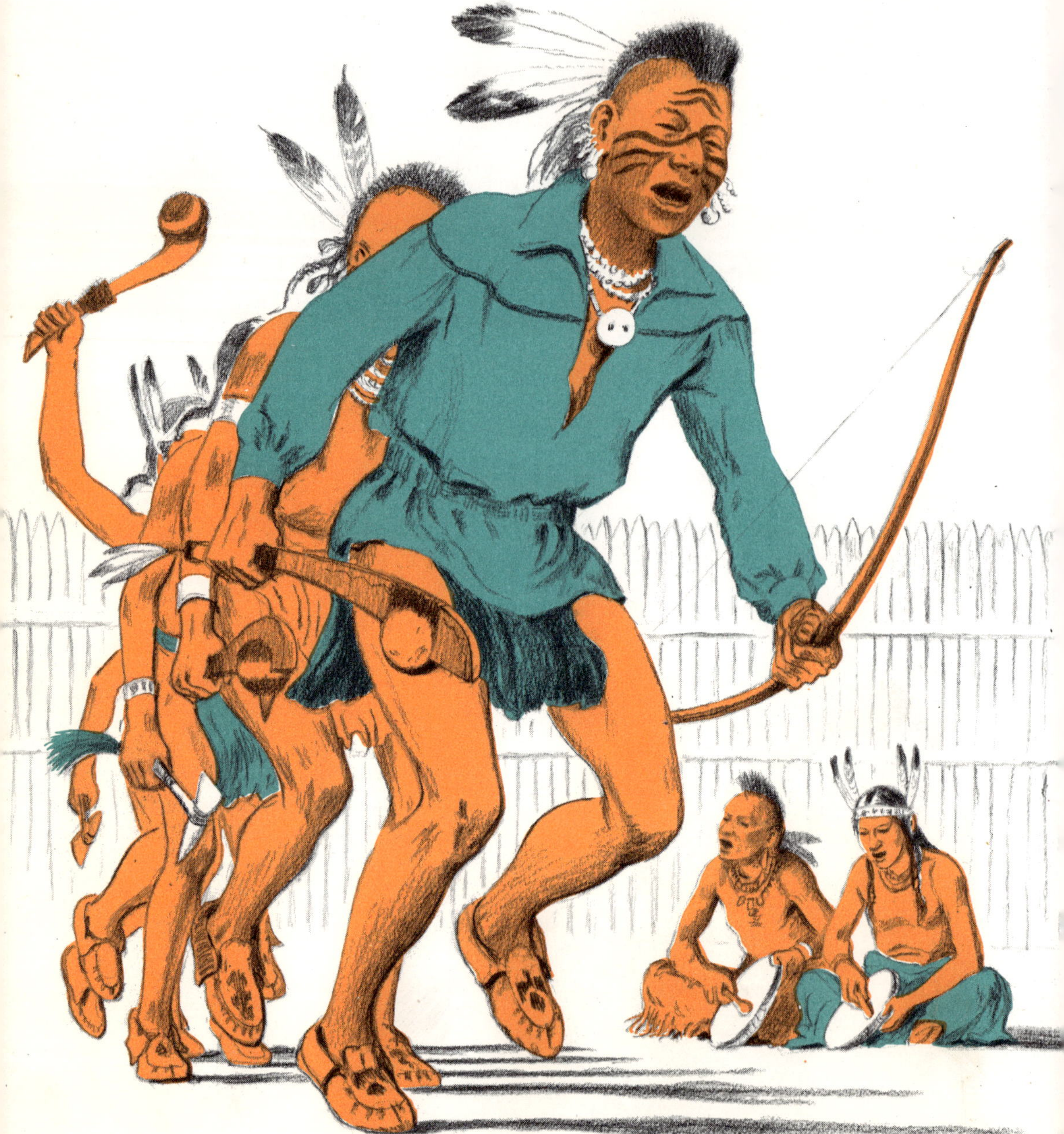

action by the friendly Indian nations had saved Detroit.

The commander at the French fort wanted to show his Indian friends how grateful he was. He gave a great feast. A few French settlers lived on farms along the Detroit River. They too were invited. One of them made a speech to the Indians.

"We thank you for your brave defense of Detroit," he said. "The northern warriors would have burned our homes and killed us all."

The feasting and dancing went on all day. Indians beat their drums. Some of the Frenchmen played on fiddles. Pontiac sang a victory song and led a line of braves in a dance. It was a happy time for everyone. All were sure that the People of the Calumet and the French would be neighbors at Detroit forever.

3
Pontiac Accepts a Red Belt

The battle with the northern warriors taught the French a lesson. They built up the fort until Detroit was one of the strongest forts in America.

"Now let our enemies come!" cried the French commander. "No one can capture this fort."

"It might be taken by surprise," Pontiac said thoughtfully.

He had come to the fort to smoke a pipe with his friend the commander.

The officer laughed. "With your help, my friend, we will make sure that no enemy surprises us. The ones to watch are the English and their American colonists. They want to take Canada away from us, and they will steal your lands as well, if they can."

Pontiac already knew that the tribes in Pennsylvania and the Ohio Valley were having trouble with the English settlers. Messengers from those Indian nations had brought word to the Ottawa village.

"More and more settlers are pouring across the mountains and into our hunting grounds," the messengers complained. "They cut down the trees and build cabins on our land. Soon we will have no place to hunt."

"It will go hard with the English if they try to steal Ottawa land!" Pontiac told them angrily. "We will not have any white men at Detroit except our French brothers. The French live among us as friends. They seem almost like our own people."

Many years before Pontiac was born, the French had come to America and settled in Canada. They built fortified trading posts and small villages along the St. Lawrence River and the Great Lakes. Everywhere, they made friends with the Indians and promised not to take their lands. Now they were building new forts along the Ohio River and the Mississippi.

"We will keep this country wild forever," they told the different tribes. "It will always be full of fur-bearing animals. You will live here as you have always done, and the fur trade between us will be good for both of us."

The English colonies were in what is today the eastern part of the United States. They stretched from the Atlantic Ocean to the Allegheny Mountains. The

English also wanted to control the rich fur trade with the Indians, but they thought it was even more important to clear land for farms and settlements. They angered the tribes by cutting down the forest. They frightened away the animals on which the Indians depended for food and clothing.

One day in 1754, Pontiac heard about a new fort France had built in western Pennsylvania. It stood where two rivers flowed together to form the great Ohio.

"We call it Fort Duquesne," a French officer told him. "It will stop any more English from moving west."

The following spring some Delaware Indians from Pennsylvania came to the Ottawa village. Pontiac met with them in the council house. He was now one of the leading chiefs in the nation. They smoked a pipe together. Then the chief of the Delawares handed Pontiac a belt of red wampum beads.

Wampum belts were used to send messages from nation to nation. They were like white men's letters. A red belt meant war.

"The French chief at Fort Duquesne sends this belt to you," the Delaware said. "These are the words it brings. 'The king of England is sending a large army to capture Fort Duquesne. There are only a few soldiers here. We need the help of our Ottawa brothers. Take up your hatchets and come!'"

"We will answer the call of our French brother," Pontiac promised.

That night he led a war dance in the Ottawa village. The next morning a large war party started down the long trail to Fort Duquesne. Pontiac's face was painted for war with lines of red and black. He wore two eagle feathers in his scalp lock, and he carried a fine French gun.

The Ottawa camp was set up outside the walls of Fort Duquesne. Close to it were the camps of the Chippewa, Potawatomie, and Huron warriors. Farther away were the Delaware and Shawnee camps. All these nations felt that they could best save their hunting grounds by siding with the French.

Pontiac's fame as a war chief had spread to other nations. He was made welcome in all the camps.

"We must fight hard," he kept saying. "The English must be stopped before they steal all our land."

Pontiac was a powerful speaker. The men of the other nations listened to him with respect. They believed that he was wise at the council fire, as well as brave in battle.

4
The Battle at Fort Duquesne

Indian scouts brought word to Fort Duquesne that the English army was getting close. The French knew that the English were commanded by a famous general named Braddock. One day in July an Ottawa scout raced into Pontiac's camp.

"The English are camped only eight miles down the trail!" he shouted.

Now that the English were so close, some French officers did not want to fight.

"The enemy greatly outnumbers us,"

said one man. "Let us burn the fort and go to Canada."

"No! Let us fight to the end!" cried brave young Captain Beaujue.

"My warriors and I will stay here and fight," Pontiac promised. "We will hide along the trail and spring on the English like a panther on a deer!"

The chiefs of the other Indian nations said that they would fight also.

Pontiac and his warriors cleaned their guns, sharpened their knives, and painted their faces. When all was ready, they hurried to the gate of the fort.

The French rolled out barrels of gunpowder and bullets and invited the Indians to help themselves. Warriors from all the nations crowded about to fill their deerskin bags. Then they silently disappeared into the forest. With them went Captain Beaujue and 200 French soldiers.

Pontiac led the Ottawa war party down a narrow trail. The English must come up this trail after they crossed the Allegheny River. Trees grew thickly on both sides. Pontiac hid his men in a woodsy hollow near the trail. The other war parties and the French hid nearby.

From down the trail came the sound of drums. There was a flash of red under the trees as the English came into sight. They were marching in perfect order. Bright flags were flying. Guns and bayonets gleamed. Officers on horseback shouted orders.

Not a sound came from the Indians and the French hidden behind trees and rocks. Each man held his gun ready. Pontiac waited until the soldiers were marching past. Then he gave the signal for the Ottawas to attack. The French and the other Indians opened fire also.

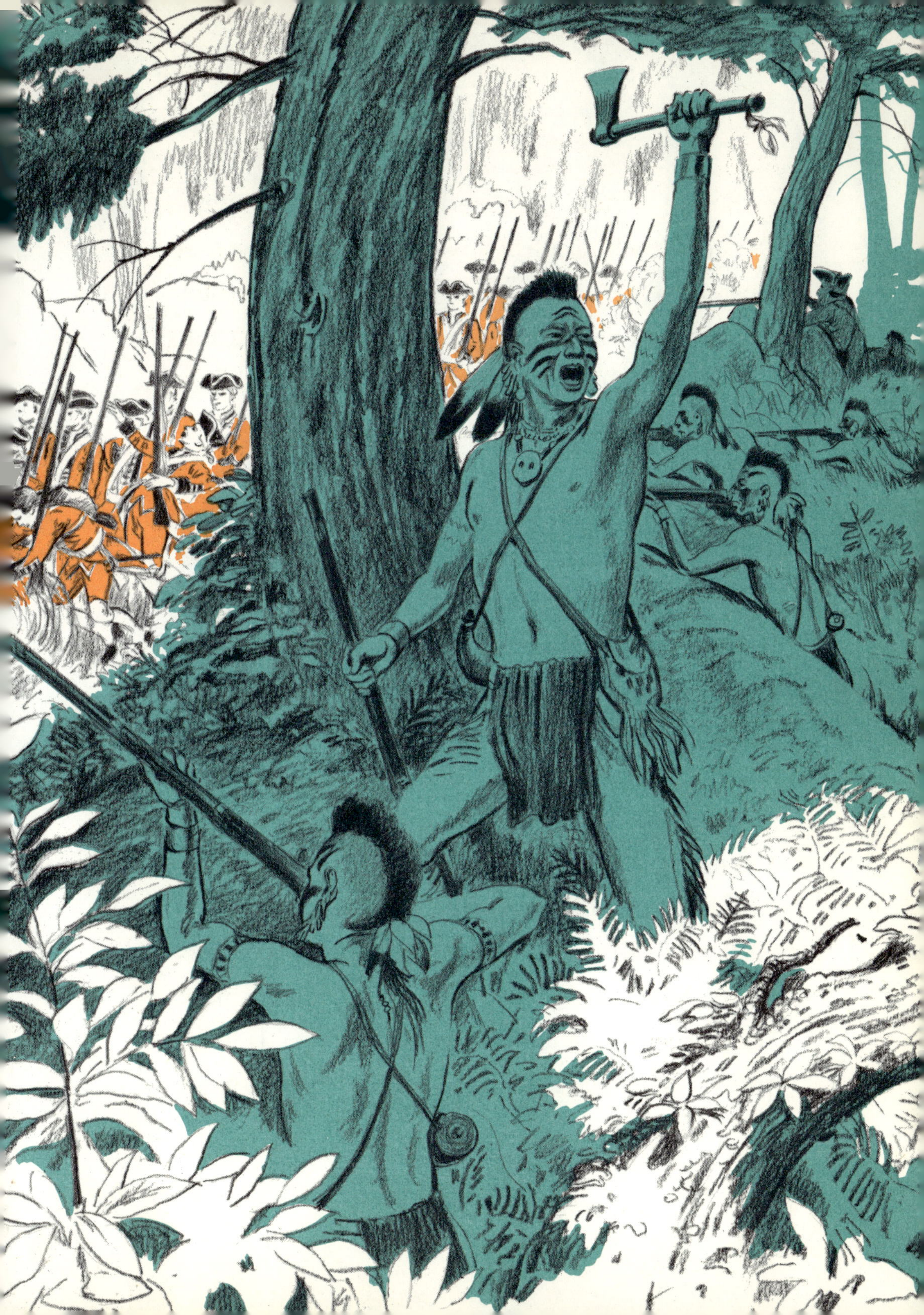

Before they realized what had happened, the English were shot down in heaps. Those who were left fired their muskets, but they could not see their enemies. Their bullets flew wild. They then charged with their bayonets, but the warriors slipped away among the trees.

Captain Beaujue was one of the first French soldiers to be killed. After that the French took only a small part in the battle. The Indian warriors carried on with their guns and hatchets. Soon a bullet knocked General Braddock off his horse. Later, word spread through the English army that he was dying. The terrified soldiers stopped fighting. They huddled in the road like sheep.

There were a few American soldiers from the colony of Virginia. These men had been trained to fight from behind trees, as the Indians did. They were commanded by a young officer named George Washington. Washington and his men fought hard to save the English army. Bullets whistled through the young officer's clothes. Two horses were shot under him. Still he was unhurt.

Pontiac fired again and again at the officer from Virginia, but every bullet missed him. At last the chief lowered his gun.

"That brave soldier is protected by the Great Spirit!" he cried. "It is useless to shoot at him."

Pontiac also was unhurt, although he stayed in the thick of the fight. This made his warriors believe that he too was protected by the Great Spirit.

Only the hard fighting by George Washington and his men kept the entire English army from being destroyed. It was a sad, small company of English that escaped back over the mountains.

5
A Meeting in the Forest

After the defeat of General Braddock, Pontiac and his warriors returned to Detroit. Fort Duquesne had been saved. But fierce fighting between the French and English still raged in the East.

The English and their colonists greatly outnumbered the French. They also had the Iroquois Indian nations for allies. General Montcalm was the French commander. He sent a red belt to the Great Lake nations at Detroit.

"Brothers, we need your help. Take up

the hatchet! Together we will drive the English into the sea."

The hottest fighting was going on around Lake Champlain and Lake George in New York. Pontiac took a large war party to join the French there. General Montcalm came to the Ottawa camp to welcome Pontiac. With him the general brought a present from the king of France. It was the white uniform of a French army officer. The uniform was richly trimmed with gold. A sword and two pistols came with it.

Pontiac was proud of his fine uniform, but in battle he always wore his deerskins and eagle feathers.

Fierce fighting continued between the two armies. Both sides won victories and suffered defeats too. During the fighting Pontiac began to change his mind about the English. At Fort Duquesne he had thought they were all cowards. But the English and colonials in this army were brave, hard-fighting men. They understood Indian warfare. And they kept pushing ever deeper into Canada.

One day, a messenger came to Pontiac's camp from Pennsylvania.

"There has been more fighting at Fort Duquesne," he told the chief. "The French lost the fort. Before they went away, they burned it. Now the English are building a strong new fort. They call it Fort Pitt."

Worse news followed. The great fortress of Quebec was captured by the English. General Montcalm was killed in the battle. Then Montreal, the last French stronghold in the East, fell.

In 1760, the Canadian government surrendered to the English. The war was over in America!

"All of Canada will now belong to England," a French officer explained to Pontiac. "So will all our forts east of the Mississippi River. We will keep only New Orleans."

Pontiac's face set in hard lines. "I will not surrender to the English!"

He told his warriors to make ready the canoes. They were going home to Detroit.

The people of the Ottawa village welcomed their brave warriors home again. Pontiac put on his fine French uniform so that all could admire it. Afterward, his wife packed it carefully away in a deerskin bag. In the future the chief would wear it only on special occasions.

Pontiac visited his old friends at Fort Detroit. The French were to remain there until the English came to take it over. That summer of 1760 the friendly life of the Ottawas and the French went on as in the past. The hated English seemed far away.

Pontiac and his sons made a new canoe. They hunted and fished, making sure that food was plentiful. The chief's wife worked with the other women in the village gardens. Their laughter and cheerful voices were good to hear. Sometimes the women went in canoes to gather wild rice along the edge of the lake.

In the evening, the Ottawas gathered to hear stories told by the old men of the village. In that way they learned the history of their nation. Sometimes they danced to the beating of drums.

Summer ended with the Green Corn Dance. This was the Ottawas' way of thanking the Great Spirit for a good harvest.

That same fall the French commander at the fort invited Pontiac to visit him.

"As you know, chief," the officer said, "we promised to give this fort to the English. Today I received a letter from Sir Jeffrey Amherst. He commands all the English soldiers in America. He is sending a company of Rangers to take over Fort Detroit. They are led by Major Rogers, a famous soldier from New England."

Pontiac knew all about Rogers' Rangers. They had been fierce fighters in Canada.

"I will go to meet this Rogers," he said. "I will make him understand that this country belongs to my people. The English can come here only if I let them come."

"The English are powerful people," warned the French officer.

"They will find that I too am powerful," Pontiac said proudly.

With a war party he started east to meet Rogers' Rangers.

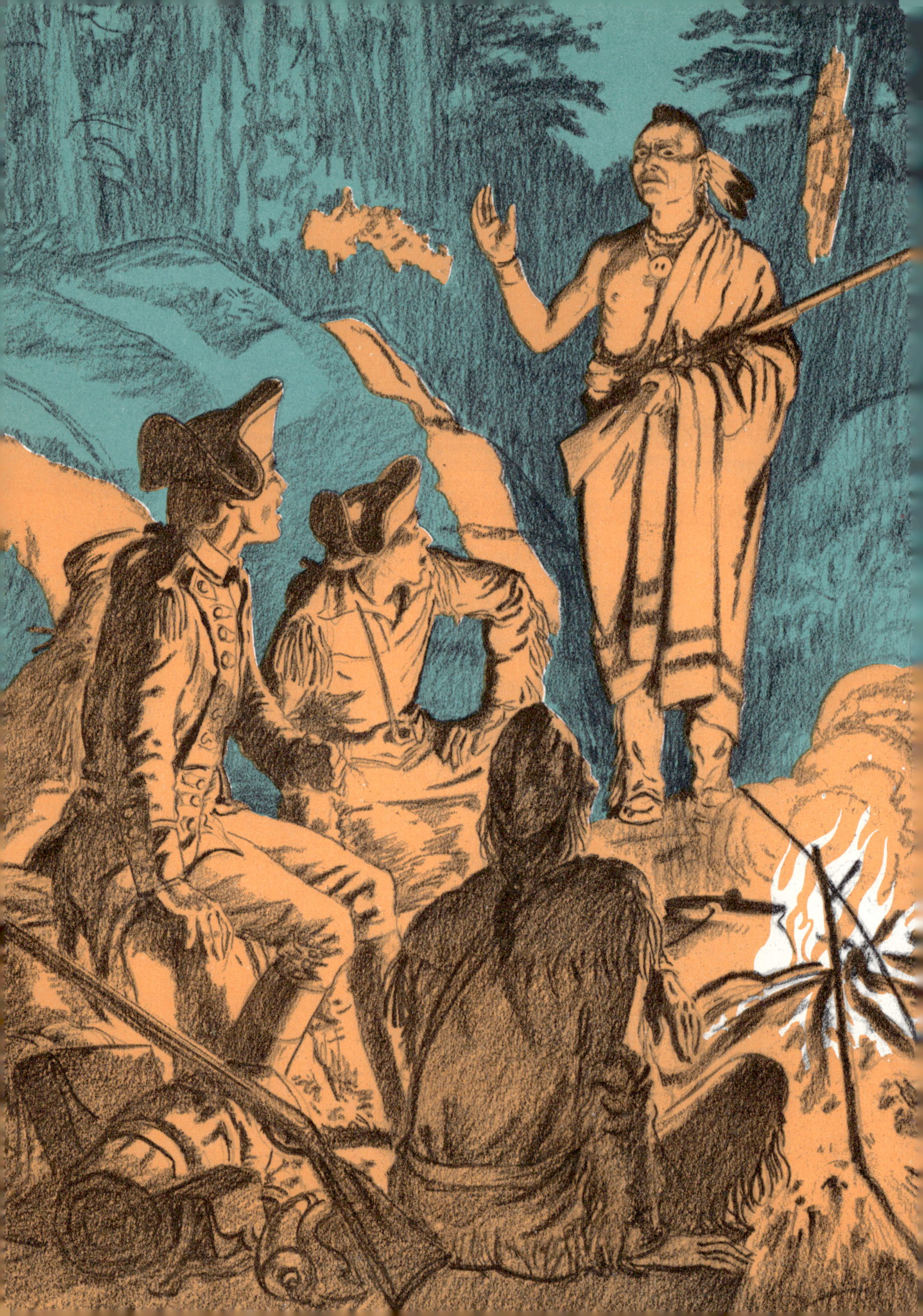

Major Rogers and his men were sailing west on Lake Erie in a number of small boats. Every night they went ashore to camp. After supper the Rangers sat around their campfires. One night the figure of an Indian appeared in the firelight. He was wrapped in a red blanket. In one hand he held a gun. He raised the other hand in greeting.

"I am Pontiac," he said in a deep voice.

Major Rogers got slowly to his feet. The other Rangers sat very still. They had heard that Pontiac was the most powerful chief in the West. Now they wondered how many warriors were behind him in the shadows.

Major Rogers was a bold man. "Welcome, Pontiac," he said calmly.

"How dare you come into my country without my permission?" Pontiac asked angrily.

"Let us talk," Rogers replied.

"I will return at sunrise," Pontiac told him. "Until then, the trail to Detroit is closed. Do not try to pass," he warned.

He disappeared into the forest.

It was an anxious night for the Rangers. They kept their guns ready, for they feared an attack. In the morning Pontiac returned with several other chiefs.

"The forts in this country belong to England now," Major Rogers told them. "General Amherst has sent me to take them over. We promise to deal fairly with your people."

Pontiac's heart was heavy. He had never liked the English. But they had won the war, and now they were making fine promises. Perhaps the People of the Calumet should try to live in peace with them. He agreed to smoke a peace pipe with Major Rogers.

"You called the king of France 'father,'" Major Rogers said. "The king of England hopes that you will call him 'father' also."

Pontiac thought about this. At last he said, "I will call your king 'uncle.'"

This meant that Pontiac would look upon the king as his equal as a chief. But he would never love and respect him as he did the king of France.

Major Rogers had to be content with that.

The following day Pontiac and his warriors stood aside and let the Rangers go on to Detroit.

6
Trouble with the English

That winter Pontiac and the other Ottawa hunters had good luck with their trapping. They returned to their summer village with heavy packs of fur. The English traders had already arrived from the East. Eagerly the hunters went to the fort to trade.

Pontiac was greatly disappointed by what the English had to offer.

"Your goods are poor, and your prices are too high," he told the trader. "Also, you offer us too little for our fur." He picked up a blanket. "You want three beaver skins or six deer skins for this. It is not worth a single beaver skin."

The trader gave him a dark look. "If you want to trade, you must pay our prices."

The Ottawas had used up all their ammunition in the winter hunt. They badly needed new supplies. They also wanted fishhooks, new knives, blankets, and other things. They were forced to sell their furs cheaply. They had to pay the high prices for the trader's goods.

This angered Pontiac. Also, he was disappointed because the king of England had sent no gifts to the Ottawas. It had been different in the days when the French were at the fort. They had given many gifts. Every spring they had held a great feast for the People of the Calumet. The English did none of these things.

"We are no longer welcome at Fort Detroit," Pontiac told his people. "After they get our furs, the English order us to leave."

Pontiac complained to the English commander at the fort. "The king of England is a mean, unfriendly fellow. He sends no gifts. His traders cheat my people. Times were better for us when the French were here."

"The French are gone. We are in command now," the officer said. "You must accept our way of doing things."

The old hatred for the English boiled up inside Pontiac. He went alone into the forest to think about what he should do. As he walked beneath the great trees, his heart was full of love for his beautiful country. He loved the green trees with their singing birds. He loved the clear river and the sparkling blue water of the lake. Except for his friends the French, he did not want white people living here.

Someday, he was sure, the French would return to the lake country. But for now, their trading posts were closed, and his people must trade with someone. They had come to depend more and more on things sold to them by white traders.

"My father was right. We should have held fast to the old ways of our people," Pontiac thought sadly. "Now it is too late. Most of our men have forgotten how to make bows and arrows. They no longer make bone needles. The women ask for steel needles. They want cloth instead of deerskin for dresses. The children cry for white men's toys." He shook his head sadly. "There is no other way. We must trade with the English until the French return."

Soon after this, two Frenchmen from New Orleans came to the Ottawa village. They were dressed as Indians so the English would not know they were there. Pontiac welcomed them to his wigwam. His wife set bowls of meat and rice before them.

"We miss our French brothers," Pontiac told his guests. "Times have changed since they went away. We are always short of ammunition for hunting. The English allow us to buy very little."

"They keep you short so you will not be able to fight when they attack you. The English are planning to wipe out all Indians. They want to divide your land among English settlers."

Pontiac frowned. Then he asked the question that was always in his mind. "If we go on the warpath against the English, will French soldiers help us?"

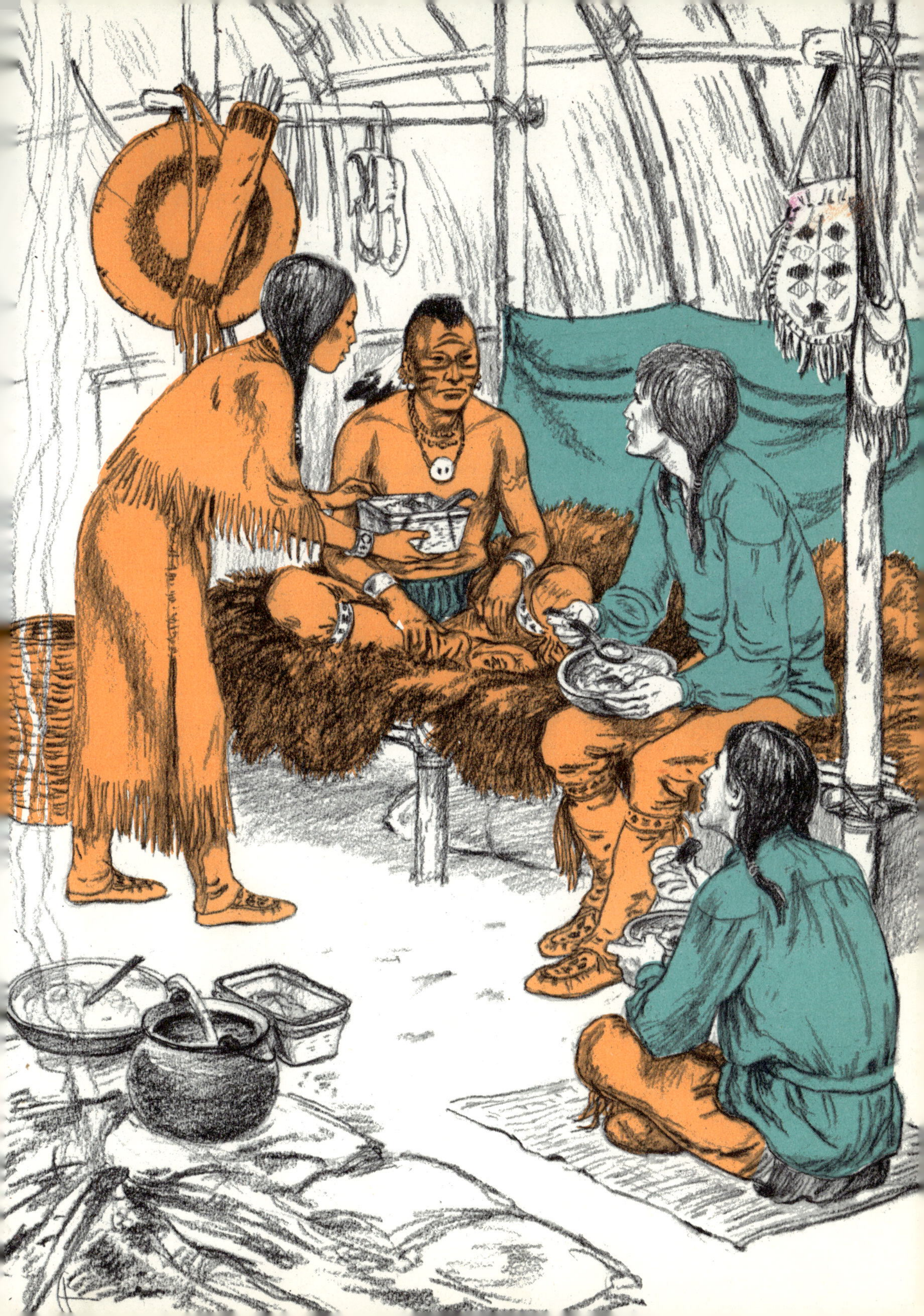

"They will come after you start fighting," the Frenchmen promised.

The men had no right to make such a promise. France and England had made peace. This was bad for the French traders. These two had come to stir Pontiac's people up to fight again. If war came and Pontiac won, French traders would again control the rich fur trade in America.

Soon after the Frenchmen went away, Pontiac had two more visitors. They were Seneca chiefs from New York. They too were boiling with anger against the English.

"General Amherst is taking our land and giving it to his soldiers," they told Pontiac. "Soon we will have no place to hunt. Our only chance to save our hunting grounds is to go on the warpath."

Delaware and Shawnee messengers from the Ohio country brought the same sort of stories. As he listened, Pontiac grew more and more angry. He was sure now that he must make war on the English.

Once more he went into the forest to think. There, in the green stillness, a great plan came to him.

He would try to unite every nation in the Great Lakes and the Ohio Valley. Under his leadership, they would fight their common enemy, the English. They would drive the English away.

It was a bold plan that had never been tried before. Each Indian nation had always made war or peace as it pleased. No chief had ever led all of them together. But Pontiac believed that he could make his plan work.

And the sooner he got on with it the better.

7
War Plans

In the spring of 1763, Pontiac held a secret meeting in the forest. Chiefs of the Ottawa, Chippewa, Potawatomie, and Huron nations met with him around a council fire.

"The time has come for us to take up the hatchet," Pontiac told them. "If we want to keep our country, we must cut the English down. I will ask every nation east of the Mississippi to join us. The English dogs will not be strong enough to stand against all of us together."

He held his hatchet high. The firelight

sparkled on its blade. "Who will follow me on the warpath?"

One by one the other chiefs spoke in favor of the plan.

"Not a whisper of our plans must reach the English," Pontiac warned them. "When we strike, we must take them by surprise."

He sent a red hatchet and a red war belt to each Indian nation east of the Mississippi. To every chief his messengers repeated his plan.

"We will strike on the day when the moon changes. On that day let each nation fall upon the nearest English fort or settlement. Every one of the English must be killed or taken prisoner. Next we will carry the war to the East. We will wipe out all of the settlements there. Then we will be free of the English forever!"

Pontiac himself would lead the attack on Detroit, the strongest English fort.

Everywhere in the many Indian villages, people listened to the Ottawa messenger. Chiefs and warriors promised to join Pontiac. Never before had so many been willing to follow one chief. The men made ready their weapons. French traders sent guns and ammunition secretly from New Orleans. The English did not dream that war was coming.

Pontiac wanted to capture Fort Detroit with as little harm as possible to his own men. To do this he must take the English by surprise. He asked Major Gladwin to meet him and some of his warriors in council at the fort. His warriors would carry guns under their blankets. Once inside the fort, they would whip out the guns and shoot down every Englishman.

On the morning of May 6, the wife of an English settler went to the Ottawa village to buy some deer meat. She saw warriors cutting down their guns so they could be easily hidden. Others were sharpening knives and hatchets. Suddenly she felt afraid. Something strange was going on! But she pretended not to have seen a thing. She paid for the meat and went away quickly.

Once she was outside the village, she ran to the fort to tell Major Gladwin what she had seen.

That night an Indian woman who knew the major warned him that Pontiac was going to attack.

There were not many soldiers at the fort, but the major was a brave man. He would try to fool Pontiac into believing that Detroit was stronger than it really was.

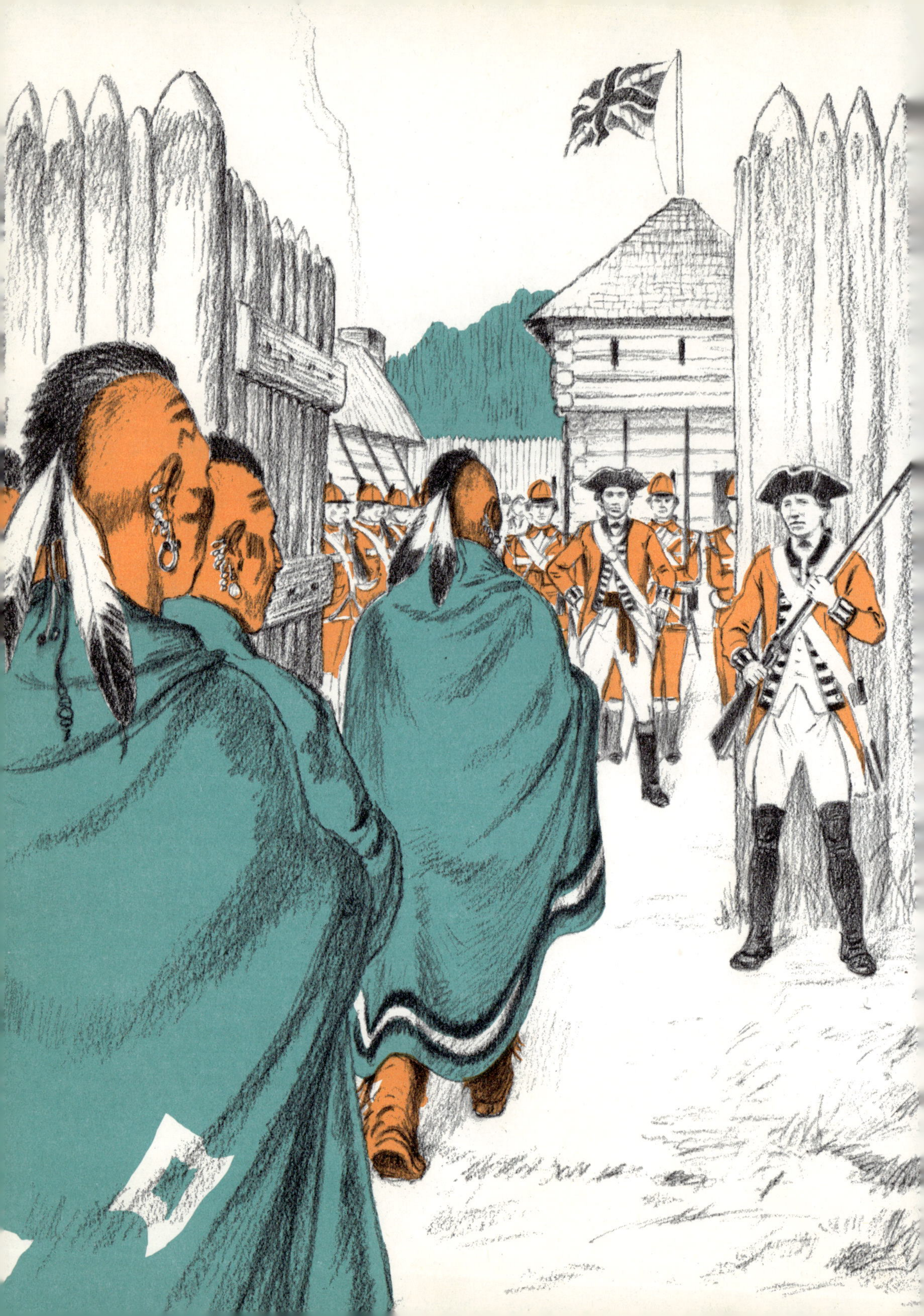

On the morning of May 7, 1763, Pontiac appeared at the fort gate with 300 warriors. Every man had a gun hidden under his blanket.

The gate stood open, but to Pontiac's surprise, there were more soldiers around than usual. All of the men were heavily armed.

Outside Major Gladwin's house, the major and some other officers were waiting. Their faces were cold and hard as they greeted the chief. It seemed plain to Pontiac that his plan had been discovered. He could not take the fort by surprise!

He did not give the signal for his warriors to shoot. It would mean that many of them would be killed. The English soldiers walled them in.

Walking tall and straight, Pontiac led his warriors back to the Ottawa village.

8
A Victory for Pontiac

"We failed to surprise the redcoats today," Pontiac told his people. "But I have made a new plan. Food and gunpowder are low at the fort. We will make sure that the supply boat from Fort Niagara never arrives. When the English are hungry enough, they will give in."

He set men to watching the fort day and night. No one could get in or out. A few English settlers were now living near the fort. Pontiac sent warriors to burn their cabins. Some settlers were killed. Others were made prisoners.

"Do not harm our French friends," the chief warned his men.

He himself visited the French settlers. The English had allowed most of them to keep their farms. "I will protect you," Pontiac told them, "if you do not try to take food to the fort."

Pontiac bought food from the French farmers. He paid for it with notes written on birchbark. The notes promised that the farmers would be paid in money, later. The chief signed the notes with his mark, a raccoon.

Warriors in canoes kept watch on the river and on Lake Erie. One day they captured some boats bringing supplies from Fort Niagara in New York. Pontiac divided the food, guns, and ammunition among the different Indian villages, and he had some captured flags waved outside the fort.

Soon there were other English flags to wave in victory. At every English fort in the lake country, Pontiac's plans for capture were successful. In the Ohio Valley, also, his plans brought victory to Indian war parties. Every fort there, except Fort Pitt, was captured.

At Detroit, the English were now very hungry. Still they held out. Pontiac realized that it would take a long time to starve them into surrender. He could not storm the walls without losing a great many warriors. Such a loss of life would be against the war customs of his people. A chief was supposed to win victories without getting many warriors killed.

Pontiac tried to burn the fort by shooting fire arrows over the walls. That too failed.

The fort had been built by white soldiers. "Perhaps," Pontiac thought, "a white officer could tell me how to capture it."

There was still a French fort in Illinois. Pontiac sent a runner with a message to the commanding officer.

"My father," the message went, "send me a French officer who is skilled in white men's warfare."

He also asked for someone who could teach his people how to make and repair guns.

Day after day he waited. No French officer came to help him.

On the night of July 28th, a thick fog covered the Detroit River. Through the fog, silent as ghost ships, some English boats moved upstream. They had been sent by General Amherst. They were carrying supplies and soldiers to Fort Detroit.

Too late, some Huron warriors saw the

boats. They fired and killed some soldiers, but the boats got through to the fort. Wild cheering broke out when the soldiers landed. They were commanded by Captain James Dalyell.

Captain Dalyell knew nothing about fighting Indians, but he made plans for an attack on Pontiac's village.

Major Gladwin shook his head. "You will never surprise that foxy chief," he warned.

Captain Dalyell went ahead with his plans.

The moon shone brightly on the night of July 30th. One of Pontiac's French friends was watching the fort. Suddenly he saw the gate swing open. Captain Dalyell's redcoats marched out. On the river road they turned toward Pontiac's village.

It was lucky for Pontiac that the

Frenchman was a fast runner. He reached the village well ahead of the soldiers.

"Chief, the soldiers are coming!" he cried.

Pontiac called his warriors together. He divided them into two bands.

At the beginning of the war, Pontiac had moved his village to the same side of the river as the fort. To reach it from the road, Dalyell must cross a narrow bridge over a stream. Pontiac had one warrior band hide near the bridge. He sent the second band across the bridge.

"Go through the woods and get behind the redcoats," he ordered. "We will stay here and open fire when they reach the bridge. When you hear our guns, shoot at them from the rear. Between our two fires, the English will fall like trees in a hurricane."

The English came marching along the road in the moonlight.

"Hold your fire until they are on the bridge," Pontiac told his men. His eyes burned with hate for the invaders of his country.

Tramp! Tramp! Tramp! The bridge echoed to the sound of marching feet. Now it was crowded with soldiers. This was the time for the warriors to strike! Pontiac gave the signal, and a blaze of gunfire swept the bridge. Almost every soldier on it was shot down. More soldiers ran up to help their comrades. Hot and heavy fighting followed. Many wounded men fell into the stream. The water ran red with their blood.

Ever after, this stream would be called Bloody Run, in memory of this battle.

The warrior band behind the English had also made its attack. All along the

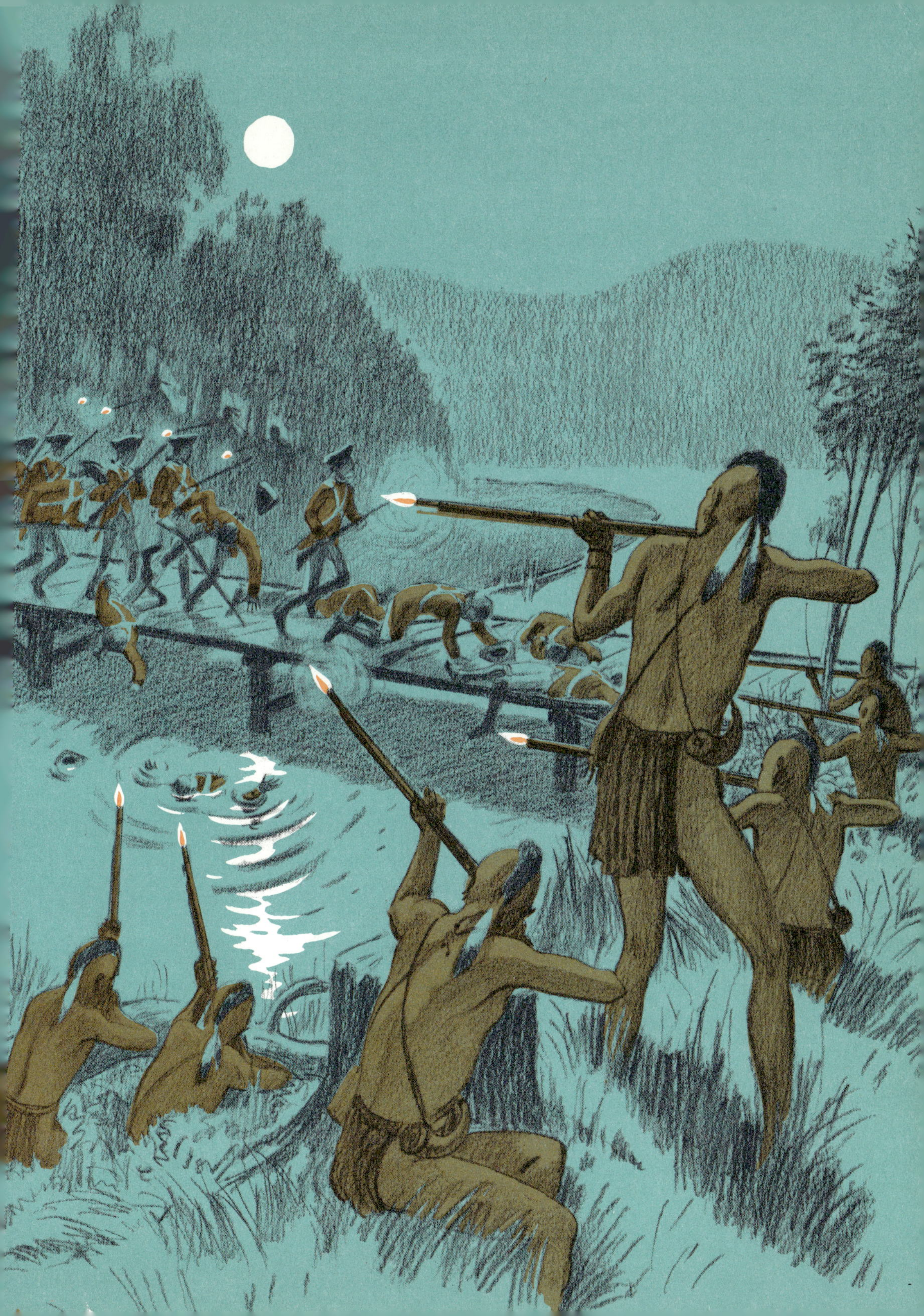

road fierce fighting was going on. The English soldiers were getting the worst of it. At last Captain Dalyell ordered a retreat.

The soldiers had to fight all the way back to the fort. Many more were killed, Captain Dalyell among them.

Pontiac lost only a few warriors.

After this Battle of Bloody Run, even the English spoke of Pontiac as a great leader. But General Amherst fell into a rage over the English defeat.

He sent out word that he would pay $2,000 to the man who would kill Pontiac.

9
Pontiac Buries the Hatchet

Fall came. Still, in spite of their defeat at Bloody Run, the English held out at Fort Detroit.

One day some chiefs met with Pontiac in the Ottawa council house. They smoked the calumet together. Then one chief told Pontiac that many of the Ottawas and Chippewas were longing for peace.

"Our people have been on the warpath all summer," he said. "No other chief but you, Pontiac, could have held us together for so long. But now our warriors are tired of fighting. We win victories, yet the English will not give in.

"Winter is coming. The men have no time to hunt. There is no meat in many wigwams. Our ammunition is running low. We must offer the peace pipe to the English."

"I will not smoke the peace pipe with those who steal our land," Pontiac said.

Yet in his heart he knew there was truth in what the other men said. His people were tired of war. There was no law to make warriors stay on the warpath. They would follow a chief of their own free will. Then, if they wished to stop fighting, they did that also.

It was almost time now for the winter hunt. Every day a few more families slipped away from the village and disappeared into the forest. Pontiac's army was getting smaller and smaller.

In the fall of 1763, a messenger brought Pontiac a letter. It was from the commander of the French fort in Illinois.

"My friend," the letter read, "the king of France wishes you to bury the hatchet and smoke a peace pipe with the English."

That night Pontiac sat a long time alone by the fire. His heart was heavy. He realized now that he could never expect help from France.

A few chiefs went to the fort to talk peace with Major Gladwin. "There can be no real peace," the major said, "unless Pontiac agrees."

Once more the chiefs met with Pontiac.

"For the good of our people, smoke the peace pipe," they pleaded.

Pontiac looked at them in heavy silence. He believed that if he gave in, his country would be lost forever. Yet he knew that his people wanted peace. At last he answered in a deep, sad voice. "I will smoke a peace pipe."

He sent a message to Major Gladwin. "Let us forget the bad things we have done to one another. Let us think of peace between our people."

Major Gladwin would have liked to punish Pontiac for making war, but he did not dare. Pontiac was still a powerful chief who could cause much trouble. Many warriors from many tribes would still follow him. Besides, the English wanted the war to end. They had lost many more men than the Indians had. So Gladwin advised General Amherst to accept Pontiac's offer of peace. There should be no punishment of any kind for the great Ottawa chief, he said.

Pontiac kept the peace, but his feelings toward the invaders of his country did not change. He wanted to get as far away as possible from the English. For a while he and his people wandered about. Finally they settled on a beautiful island in the Maumee River in Indiana.

Great trees shaded their comfortable village. Corn grew high in the rich earth. The men found good hunting and fishing. The women talked and laughed as they sat in front of their wigwams and made baskets. The children played happily on the river bank. It was like the good village life before the war.

In the fall of 1765, Pontiac was invited to Fort Oswego in New York. There he met Sir William Johnson, the king of England's Indian agent. Although Pontiac had stopped fighting, he had never signed a peace treaty. Sir William asked him to sign one now.

At Oswego Pontiac saw how strong the

English had become. He believed that it would be best for his people if he signed the treaty.

"I am willing for you to have forts and trading posts in my country," he told Sir William. "But English settlers must stay off our lands."

Sir William promised that the settlers would stay away. To seal the treaty, he hung a big silver medal around Pontiac's neck. On it was written, "A pledge of Peace and Friendship, 1766."

Pontiac was glad to get away from the English and return to his village on the Maumee River. Two Miami chiefs from the Ohio Valley soon visited him there.

"The English settlers are moving west in greater numbers than ever," they told him.

"Then Sir William's promises were only words!" Pontiac said angrily.

"Our people in the Ohio Valley are fighting to turn the settlers back," one of the chiefs said. "We need a leader. Take up the hatchet again, Pontiac, and lead us."

"I will never again make war on the English," Pontiac answered sadly. "They are too many for us, and they get stronger every day." He thought a moment and then spoke again. "Perhaps our people should move west of the Mississippi River. Across the Father of Waters, there are no English."

"No! We will stay and fight," the Miami said.

After the chiefs had gone, Pontiac thought often about moving west. He knew that the French had built a new fort on the west bank of the Mississippi. They called the little settlement St. Louis. It stood on ground to which England had no claim.

"It would be good to live near our French friends again," Pontiac told his sons.

In the spring of 1769, Pontiac started out with his family and a small band of warriors. Captain Louis St. Ange was the French officer in command at St. Louis. He gave Pontiac a warm welcome. For this meeting the chief wore his white and gold French uniform.

"My heart is still French," he told the captain

The following day, Pontiac heard that there was to be a big Indian powwow, or gathering. It would be held in a village across the river. He decided to go and join in the feasting and dancing.

Captain St. Ange begged him not to go. "There are English traders across the river who hate you, Pontiac. Stay here, my friend, where I can protect you."

Pontiac laughed. "I have no fear of English traders."

With only a few warriors, he went back across the river to English land. They found the village crowded with Indians of many nations. Pontiac took part in the dancing to the beating of drums. English traders passed out cups of rum. Some Indians drank a great deal and became quarrelsome.

A trader named Williamson watched Pontiac with eyes that burned with hate. He remembered that he and the Ottawa chief had met before. Pontiac had called him a cheat, and he had driven him out of the Ottawa village.

Near Williamson stood an Illinois Indian who was drunk. The trader led him to one side. "Would you like to have a keg of rum for yourself?" he whispered.

The Illinois nodded eagerly.

"Kill Pontiac and the rum is yours," Williamson promised.

The Illinois touched the knife in his belt and nodded.

The powwow had become more and more noisy. Pontiac grew tired of the dancing and drum-beating. He left the village and walked along a woodland trail. It was good to be alone in the cool, quiet forest!

He walked slowly, looking up at the stars shining above the treetops. He did not know that a man was sneaking along behind him. He did not see a long knife flash in the moonlight. But he felt a hard blow between his shoulders. It was the last thing he ever felt! The knife blade had pierced his heart.

The great Pontiac fell on the trail and died alone in the forest he loved.

The Illinois ran away as soon as he

struck the blow. He was terrified because of what he had done. He dared not go back to the powwow to collect his rum. Instead, he set out through the night for his own village. He tried hard to cover his tracks, but the next day Pontiac's enraged warriors found his trail. They stormed into the Illinois village. They killed the man who had murdered their chief.

Pontiac's family took his body back to St. Louis. Captain St. Ange buried him there with the honors of war. So in the end, Pontiac slept close to the French friends he loved.

The great Ottawa chief would be remembered for the fight he had put up to save his country and for his success in uniting many strong, independent Indian nations in a common cause. No other Indian chief had ever been so powerful.